Ladybugs

by Kris Bonnell

Here is a ladybug.

A ladybug is also called a ladybird or a ladybeetle.

Most ladybugs are red and black.

A ladybug is red so that other animals can see it. Most animals do not like to eat ladybugs.

A ladybug lays small yellow eggs.
Red ladybugs do not come out of the eggs.

Black bugs come out of the eggs.
The black bugs become red ladybugs.

Ladybugs have legs.
They can climb.

Ladybugs have wings.
They can fly.

Ladybugs eat very small bugs.

A girl ladybug is called a ladybug.

A boy ladybug is called a ladybug, too.